Arctic Culture
The People of the Ice

BY DIANE BAILEY

EXPLORING THE POLAR REGIONS TODAY

EXPLORING THE POLAR REGIONS TODAY

ARCTIC CULTURE
The People of the Ice

BY DIANE BAILEY

MASON CREST

Mason Crest
450 Parkway Drive, Suite D
Broomall, PA 19008
www.masoncrest.com

Printed and bound in the United States of America.

First printing
1 3 5 7 9 8 6 4 2

Series ISBN: 978-1-4222-3863-9
ISBN: 978-1-4222-3866-0
ebook ISBN: 978-1-4222-7921-2

Library of Congress Cataloging-in-Publication Data on file with the publisher.

Developed and Produced by Shoreline Publishing Group.
Developmental Editor: James Buckley, Jr.
Design: Tom Carling, Carling Design Inc.
Production: Sandy Gordon
www.shorelinepublishing.com
Front cover: Shutterstock/Bikerlondon

QR Codes disclaimer:

CONTENTS

Key Icons to Look For

 Words to Understand: These words with their easy-to-understand definitions will increase the reader's understanding of the text, while building vocabulary skills.

 Sidebars: This boxed material within the main text allows readers to build knowledge, gain insights, explore possibilities, and broaden their perspectives by weaving together additional information to provide realistic and holistic perspectives.

 Educational Videos: Readers can view videos by scanning our QR codes, providing them with additional educational content to supplement the text. Examples include news coverage, moments in history, speeches, iconic moments, and much more!

 Text-Dependent Questions: These questions send the reader back to the text for more careful attention to the evidence presented here.

 Research Projects: Readers are pointed toward areas of further inquiry connected to each chapter. Suggestions are provided for projects that encourage deeper research and analysis.

 Series Glossary of Key Terms: This back-of-the-book glossary contains terminology used throughout this series. Words found here increase the reader's ability to read and comprehend higher-level books and articles in this field.

INTRODUCTION

The Arctic seems like a forbidding place. It's covered in ice and snow, and there's no daylight for months out of the year. Plus, it's really cold. Sure, polar bears and seals have what it takes to live here. But how do humans survive in this kind of environment?

In fact, people have lived here for thousands of years. To them, the Arctic might be demanding, but it is also home. They understand what it has to offer, and know how to take advantage of it.

What do you see if you think of someone who lives in the Arctic? You might picture a hunter dressed in a fur-lined parka and boots. Maybe he's sliding across the ice on a dogsled, or paddling along in a kayak. Maybe he's warming his hands over a small fire inside an igloo.

These images are typical for traditional Arctic lifestyles, but they are becoming rare today. About four million people live in the Arctic, but only about 10 percent of them are native to the region and an even smaller fraction still live the way their ancestors did. Instead, the modern lives of many Arctic people are similar to those of people anywhere else. They live in towns and cities, drive cars, and hold regular company jobs.

These changes began centuries ago, when Europeans began to explore the Arctic. They brought their own ideas and priorities, and Arctic people had to adjust. Sometimes they did it by choice. Other times they were forced onto paths they didn't want. Either way, their lives changed—and they're still changing.

Today, Arctic people are facing new challenges. One problem is global warming. The Arctic is warming even faster than other places. The environment is being radically transformed. Technology has also made the Arctic less remote. Powerful ice-breaking ships can get where no one could before. Television and the Internet have brought in new information and culture. Meanwhile, countries all over the world are looking for ways to harvest the Arctic's natural resources.

With so many people wanting a piece of the Arctic, whose interests will come first? How much will be preserved? What will have to change with the times? Those are the big questions for people who live in the Arctic.

This stone statue represents the shape of a person. Known as an inukshuk, it has become a symbol of the people of the Arctic, especially in Canada.

The forbidding landscape of the Arctic coastline does not seem to be a fit place for humans, but people have been surviving here for thousands of years.

Moving North

1

Words to Understand

domesticate   to tame a wild animal for people to use

exiled   to be banned from a country as a punishment

indigenous   native or original to a particular place

nomadic   always moving around, often to find new food or other resources

permafrost   a layer of soil that stays frozen all year long

The common image of the Arctic is somewhat bleak. It's cold and icy, sealed in a layer of **permafrost** that never melts. It looks empty, with nothing to offer. It's true that the Arctic has vast sheets of ice, but the ice is not a solid, unmoving mass. Instead, it's almost like a living thing. It drifts, melts, and refreezes with the seasons. As it does, it brings the animals that people in the Arctic depend on for food. Polar bears travel across the ice looking for new feeding grounds. On the coastline between ice and sea there are fish, seals, and walrus. Farther inland on land that is sometimes covered with ice and snow, Arctic people hunt animals like caribou (reindeer). In the summer, thousands of birds migrate from the south. They are another important food source. The Arctic may look barren to outsiders, but it isn't that way at all. Over the millennia, there has been plenty to support the **indigenous** people who live here.

Early Inhabitants

In 2014, an 11-year-old boy in the north of Russia found something very interesting. He had stumbled on the bones of an ancient woolly mammoth. Scientists determined the mammoth had lived about 45,000 years ago. They also determined that it had not died naturally, but had been killed by humans. That meant humans had lived in the Arctic almost 50,000 years ago!

Archaeologists know more about more recent Arctic civilizations. Those people lived between 15,000 and 10,000 years ago. They began to move in large numbers into areas that now include northern Norway, Sweden, Finland, and Russia. About 5,000 years ago, people started to come to North America. Today, Russia and Alaska are separated by a channel of water called the Bering Strait. Several thousand years ago the geography was different. The sea level was much lower. Land connected the two areas. Archaeologists believe that a group of people known as Paleo-Eskimos ("old Eskimos") crossed this land bridge. They came east from the Siberian region of Russia into Alaska. Over the next several hundred years, people continued to push their way east, moving across Canada and into Greenland.

In the 1950s, archaeologists examined the remains of several ancient settlements throughout Alaska, Canada, and Greenland.

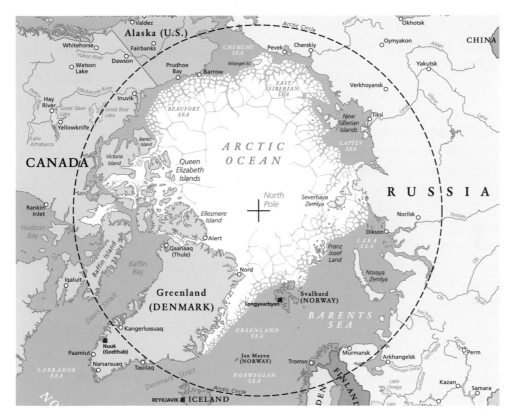

The dotted line is the Arctic Circle, which touches part of several countries. The names on the map are those of indigenous communities.

They found the people who had lived there all had things in common. Although they lived thousands of miles apart, their ways of living were very similar. They used the same kinds of tools and built the same styles of houses. Researchers concluded they came from the same cultural background. It is called the "Arctic Small Tool tradition." These people were **nomadic**. They moved with the season, looking for the best food sources. Tools such as spear blades and harpoon tips, which were small and lightweight, were designed to be easily carried.

What is an Eskimo?

It is common in the United States to use the word "Eskimo" to describe native people in Alaska and northern Canada. This is only part of the story. Eskimos also include the people who live in Arctic areas of Russia. It's not clear where the word Eskimo came from. Some think it came from a word that meant "people who eat raw meat." Others believe it means "people who wear snowshoes." Inuit people, who live throughout Canada and Greenland, are one type of Eskimo. However, they like to refer to themselves as Inuit. Inuit means "people" in their language. Other cultures, such as the Yupik in Alaska and Russia, are not Inuit—but they're still Eskimos.

The Paleo-Eskimos included a group of people called the Tunit, who later developed into a culture called the Dorset. The Dorset spread through Canada and into Greenland. The Dorset had technology such as bows and arrows that helped them survive. Their culture was somewhat unusual. For about 4,000 years, they lived almost in isolation. Stories from other Arctic cultures describe them as shy. They did not want to talk to other people.

Another group of Arctic people was the Thule. They are the ancestors of the Inuit people who still live throughout Canada and Greenland. The Thule had more advanced technology than the Dorset. They had better weapons and larger boats. This allowed them to hunt large animals like whales. They could build larger communities. After the Dorset culture died out about 1300, the Thule replaced them.

Learning to Adapt

Other people were also moving into the Arctic. About 700, the Earth started warming up during a time called the Medieval

Warm Period. Temperatures rose all over the globe. Historians think these warmer temperatures encouraged explorers to come to the Arctic region. Records show the first European explorers were the Vikings.

The Vikings were Norsemen who lived in the northern areas of Norway, Denmark, and Sweden. Many Vikings were peaceful farmers and tradesmen. That's not how they are remembered, though. Instead, their reputation is of being tough, brutal warriors who invaded communities all over Europe, taking whatever they wanted.

Erik the Red was a Viking who was always ready for a fight. He was so much trouble that even the other Vikings got fed up.

This Viking ship was found near Gokstad, Norway, and dates from about the ninth century. It was restored and is on display in Oslo.

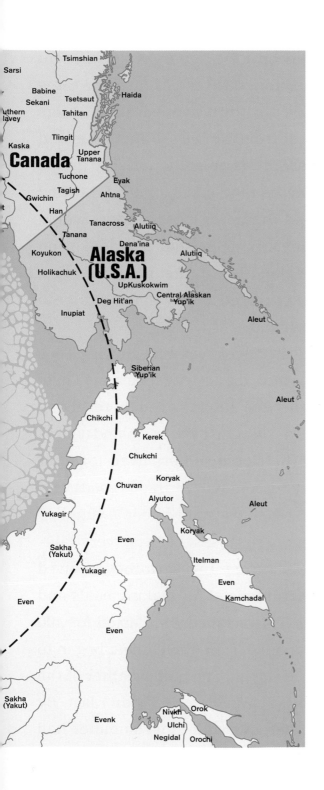

Only a few hundred thousand people today are native to the Arctic, but they are very diverse. There are more than 30 distinct indigenous groups. They speak dozens of languages. They are spread out through all 24 time zones, and over eight countries: the United States, Canada, Russia, Norway, Sweden, Finland, Iceland and Greenland (which is part of Denmark).

After Erik had killed too many people, the country of Norway sent him into **exile**. They banished him from the country for three years. They hoped he would settle down and learn his lesson. Instead, Erik sailed northwest from Norway to the icy island he named Greenland. (Greenland is actually not very green. Erik chose the name to make the land sound pretty, so more settlers would come.) Erik established a settlement on Greenland in 982. After his exile ended, he encouraged more Vikings to come to Greenland.

Soon the colonies were growing. They came into contact with the native Thule people who already lived there. Viking records show that the Greenland natives and the Norse settlers lived together fairly peacefully. They traded goods with each other. The native people supplied ivory walrus tusks that were very valuable in Europe. In return, they received wood and metal for making boats and tools. This arrangement lasted for 400 years or so. Then the climate began to change again. The mild weather of the Medieval Warm Period didn't last. By the mid-1300s, the thermometer had

Frozen in Place

The environment of the Arctic is cold and dry, which can make it a challenge to live there. But those same conditions are great for archaeologists. Heat and moisture are the enemies of most things. Animal skins, cloth, and wood decay quickly. In the Arctic, things are different. Here, the climate is tailor-made to preserve the past. Items take much longer to break down. The landscape itself also takes a long time to change. Large trees do not grow up to hide ancient settlements. There is not much soil to bury artifacts and cause them to rot. Archaeologists have an outdoor museum waiting for them. They may find tools made out of ivory from walrus tusks, the wooden shafts of spears, or clothing made from a caribou skin. All of these things would have fallen apart long ago in a warmer climate.

begun to drop. Now the Earth entered a period known as the Little Ice Age. It lasted for 300-400 years.

Under these conditions, the Norse settlers struggled. They had depended on farming and raising animals like sheep, but the cold weather made this impossible. Shorter, cooler summers, for example, would have made it too difficult to grow enough hay to feed their animals. Gradually, the Norse began to move away. By the early 1400s, they had abandoned Greenland altogether. They would not return for another 300 years.

Erik the Red is still remembered in Scandinavian countries for his far-reaching impact. This is a restoration of his house in Iceland.

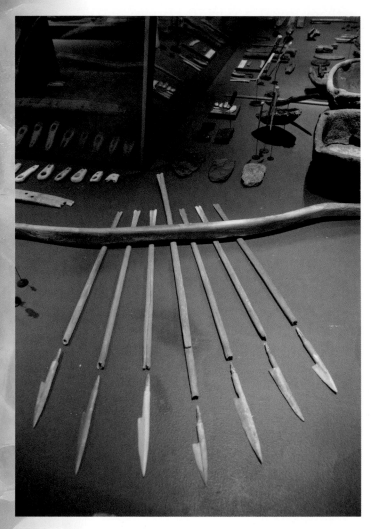

These spear points and arrows were made from whale bones and wood by the Thule people. They are displayed in a museum in Greenland.

Native Arctic people fared much better in the face of climate change. The Thule, who were spread out across Canada and Greenland, did not depend on agriculture. Their lifestyle was based on hunting and thus was much more adaptable to the cooler weather. The Thule were not tied down by having to tend crops or animals. Instead, people could move around according to the season. They could "follow the food" and change their hunting habits to match what was available. For example, when hunting bowhead whales became too difficult, the Thule switched to smaller animals like seals and fish. And instead of living in large communities, they broke into smaller ones that put less pressure on the available resources.

Reindeer Wranglers

It would be impossible to be a vegetarian in the Arctic. In some southern areas of the Arctic, people could gather a little wild food. Farther north, though, the only source of food came from animals. People who lived on the coasts fished and hunted whales, polar bears, and seals. Further inland, another animal was more important. Caribou (called reindeer in Europe and Russia) are well adapted to the Arctic environment. Their skin is covered with hollow hairs. These air-filled hairs provide extraordinary insulation against the cold. Caribou have also evolved to survive on a diet of lichen, which is similar to moss, and is one thing that grows well in the Arctic landscape. Plus, caribou are walkers. They've got tough feet, and an excellent sense of direction. They can migrate thousands of miles in a year.

In Alaska, Canada, and Greenland, caribou are wild. They are hunted by Arctic people to provide meat and fur for clothing. Several thousand miles away, the picture is much different. It began about 2,000 years ago. That's when people who lived in the areas north of Europe and Asia began to **domesticate** reindeer. They tamed them to use as pack animals to carry their belongings or as decoys to attract other animals during hunting trips. Eventually, they began to follow the reindeer herds as they traveled. They would take care of the animals and take what they needed for meat and fur.

Reindeer herding only happened in Eurasia. It did not catch on in North America. This led to a big difference in how Arctic

Even as the wider world brings changes, some Arctic people try to live in traditional ways, such as these reindeer-herding Nenets in northern Russia.

cultures in each place developed. Cultures in North America were mostly nomadic hunters. In Eurasia, they started a tradition based on raising animals. Today, reindeer herding is still an important way of life. About 100,000 people make their living this way. The Eveny in northern Siberia and the Sami in Norway are two cultures that depend on reindeer herding.

All Arctic people have had to adapt to the cold weather and challenging environment. As a result, many cultures have developed similar approaches. It is not only in how they actually do things, but also in how they think about them. Across Arctic cultures, there is a spirit of innovation, adaptation, and sharing. Those are all key to living in the Far North.

 # Text-Dependent Questions:

1. What route did Paleo-Eskimos take to move from Russia into Alaska?

2. What types of products did the Thule people of Greenland receive in trade from the Norse?

3. Name one way that people in Europe and Asia used tame reindeer to help them.

 # Research Project

Choose one of the peoples that is indigenous to the Arctic and do more research about them. How many are there? How do they live? What are some of their customs?

The Sami people

Pulled by powerful Husky dogs, sleds such as these have been used for travel by Arctic people for centuries. Today, they are also raced for sport.

Life at the Top of the World

2

Words to Understand

animism   the belief that all things have souls, including people, animals, plants and other objects

province   an area in Canada with its own name and government, similar to a state in the United States

shaman   a spiritual leader

sinew   fibers that connect muscle and bone in animals

subsistence   a basic, minimal way of living, with only things that are necessary to survive

Arctic people are often described as having a **subsistence** lifestyle. They live very basically, using the resources of the land. As a result, people in Arctic cultures are very tied to the environment. They have a deep knowledge of and respect for it.

Icy Inventions

The ice is the most obvious feature of the Arctic. Many areas are covered in ice and those that are not have still been shaped by its

While most native people have updated their gear, some still prefer to use seal skin kayaks, as shown in this photo.

movements. It builds up in the winter and melts in the summer. As it does, it pushes and pulls animal populations with it. Arctic people are very familiar with the ice and its habits. They've learned just how to live with it.

Much of the Arctic is located north of the tree line. That is where the climate becomes too cold and dry for trees to grow. People who lived here might see some occasional driftwood float through, but it wasn't enough to build houses from. Instead, they built homes from the ice and snow itself, or from the remains of animals. The famous dome shape of the igloo was formed by molding blocks of ice and packing the cracks with snow. Other ice/snow shelters took different forms depending on the location and availability of materials. In terms of animal parts, a tent, for example, might have supporting poles made of bones, with an outer layer made from a seal or caribou hide. It was also impossible to make cloth, since there were no plants to make fibers from. Clothing was also made entirely from animals. Pants, shirts, coats, and boots were all made from the furs of animals like caribou and foxes. Fishermen needed waterproof clothing, so they used the pelts of marine animals like seals.

Arctic people also figured out ways of traveling over the ice and snow. Snowshoes were invented by Arctic people. Their wide soles let people walk on top of the snow, without sinking into it. Sleds with runners that slid easily on the ice and snow were also developed in the Arctic. To pull the sleds, Arctic people also domesticated dogs like Huskies—a tough, strong, and loyal breed. They could pull heavy sleds and help in hunting expeditions. Dogsledding is still popular today. Most of the time it is just for fun, though, not work.

The kayak, which means "hunter's boat," is another Arctic invention. Kayaks were constructed by wrapping a seal skin around a driftwood frame. They were designed to easily turn back upright if they tipped over. The designs of different kayaks varied depending on where they would be used. Some were

Dogsledding in the Arctic

shorter and wider, which made them more stable on rough seas. Others were long and slender, for speed.

The Hunt

In the ancient Arctic, acquiring food was not just a chore or a routine trip to the store. Instead, everything began with the hunt.

In Arctic traditions, hunting was not a one-way act of a hunter killing his prey. It was a ritual in which both the hunter and the animal played a role. The animal's role was to allow itself to be killed. The hunter did his part by making the kill with skill and respect.

Hunting involved finding, chasing, trapping, and killing all kinds of fish and animals. There were specialized methods for each. For example, the practice of ice fishing was necessary. Fishermen would drill a hole in the ice to fish under the surface. Hunters also learned to stake out holes in the ice. There, they would wait for seals who had to come up for air. They also developed harpoon technology to kill large whales. Understanding when and where animals migrated was also important. Hunters knew how to

Nanook of the North

In the early 1920s, a film-maker named Robert Joseph Flaherty traveled to Quebec, a **province** in Canada. There, he made a movie about an Eskimo hunter named Nanook. The movie became known as the first documentary, a true story told in a film. Much of the movie, however, was not strictly fact. The hunter who played Nanook was actually named Allakariallak. The woman who played his wife was not even related to him. Scenes that showed Nanook hunting with a spear were also made up. Allakariallak was a hunter, but he used a rifle. Nonetheless, the movie was enormously popular at the time. It gave many people their first glimpse into the traditional ways in which Arctic people lived.

The Inupiaq of Alaska are among the few Arctic people that still practice the traditional art of whale hunting, working as a group.

follow the walrus, who followed the seal, who followed the fish brought north in the summer on warm ocean currents.

Every person in a family or band contributed to the hunt in some way. Men did the actual hunting, while boys learned to make weapons and looked forward to the day they were old enough to join their fathers and uncles on a hunt. Women and girls took care of preparing and preserving food. They also made clothing from the animal remains.

This Canadian postage stamp (bilingual in French and English) features a whalebone carving that depicts the Inuit sea goddess Sedna.

Spiritual rituals and celebrations were tied to the bounty of the hunt. In the Inuit tradition, for example, Sedna is the goddess of the sea. Long ago, Sedna's father threw her off a boat because she had caused trouble in the family. When she tried to climb back on, her father cut off her fingers to stop her. Her fingers turned into seals, walruses, and whales, and Sedna sank to the bottom of the sea, where she now rules over all its creatures. Although several versions of the story exist, the common theme is that Sedna is an angry goddess who holds grudges. She only allows hunters to take animals from the sea if she wants to. Hunters knew they had to keep her happy and recognize her power. They always gave back part of what they caught to Sedna.

A Place for Everyone

Arctic people knew there was one key thing that would help keep them alive. It was not the sharpest tools or the strongest dogs. It wasn't the warmest clothes or the snuggest homes. It wasn't even the most food. It was the fact that they could count on one another. The ideas of helping and sharing are important throughout Arctic cultures.

The environment of the Arctic is not good for supporting large communities. Resources are just spread out too thinly. Instead, Arctic people tended to live in small bands. There might be only a few dozen people, or a few hundred at most. Within those bands, the focus was on

Playing the Game

Young Arctic athletes today can compete in the Arctic Winter Games. This event was first held in Canada in 1970, and now happens every two years. Athletes from the United States, Canada, Greenland, and Russia have all participated. Athletic events include skiing, snowshoeing, and ice hockey. There are also some more unusual "Arctic sports" that come from the survival techniques used by ancient Arctic people. One is the "knuckle hop," in which athletes hop along the ground on their toes and knuckles. Another is "kick the seal," in which they kick a stuffed seal toy hanging from a rope eight feet off the ground. The "head pull" is like a tug-of-war between two athletes linked together by a band around their heads. For the "finger pull," two contestants link middle fingers. Then they pull until one of them pulls the other person's finger to his chest. It's more dangerous than it sounds. One competitor lost his finger that way!

the immediate family. The brothers and sisters of a family, along with their spouses, often lived close to one another, or even in the same household. The idea of kin was important to many Arctic societies. It was expected that families would take care of their own. However, there was some flexibility in who qualified as a family member. Outsiders could be added to a family if it was for the good of everyone. Someone with the same last name, or someone who was a trading partner, could be treated as a family member if it was beneficial.

Arctic people knew that everyone in a society had a job to do. Men and women performed traditional, separate tasks, but both genders were treated relatively equally. In some cultures, a specific individual served as a band's official leader, but others did not have that much structure.

Overall, people were valued based on the contributions they could make. Elderly people, for example, brought life experience. They had been through more than anyone else and their knowledge and insight were useful to everyone. Children were equally important, because they represented the future. As soon as they were old enough, children began to learn the skills they would need as adults. They were taught traditional hunting skills as well as how to survive in the harsh climate.

Children's toys, games, and sports all prepared them to contribute later in life. For example, boys needed to develop strength and agility for hunting. A great way to do this was by playing football (using walrus skulls). Girls enjoyed a game of cat's cradle using string made from animal **sinew**. This made their fingers nimble for sewing.

The Spirit World

Most Arctic cultures believed in some form of **animism**. This is the belief that all things in nature, including animals and plants, have souls. These spirits were everywhere. They played an important part in how daily life went. Happy spirits brought good fortune, but angry ones would punish people. It was important to show respect for the spirits in order to avoid trouble.

To many Arctic people, the spectacular Northern Lights (aurora borealis) represented the spirit world appearing to humans.

This late 19th-century photo shows a Nunivak man wearing fur robes and a ceremonial mask, meaning he was perhaps a shaman.

Societies were built on a complex set of beliefs, rules, and taboos that said what people could and could not do. These ranged from rituals connected to hunting—like appeasing Sedna—down to children's games. For example, it was important not to play cat's cradle during the darkness of winter. Then, there was the danger that the sun might get tangled up in the string and never return.

Everyone in a society was tied to the spirits to some degree, but some people, called **shamans**, had a special connection.

Shamans were able to put themselves into a mental trance that would take them to the world of the spirits. There, they could communicate with the spirits and find out what they wanted. Shamans could also be healers. When people got sick, it was believed to be the work of evil or angry spirits. Shamans knew what to do to make them better.

The lifestyles of Arctic people, so deeply tied to the environment, had developed over centuries. They began to be put in danger about 500 years ago, when Europeans started to push more aggressively into Arctic regions. The result was a culture clash of ideas and lifestyles. It continues to affect Arctic people today.

 # Text-Dependent Questions:

1. Name one way dogs helped in Arctic cultures.
2. What was one game played by children?
3. What was one job of a shaman?

 # Research Project

The story of Sedna is one of many myths in Arctic cultures. Look up some other stories that are part of Arctic folklore. How do the stories help describe or explain some part of their life?

American explorer Robert Peary was allegedly among the first to reach the North Pole, a feat he said happened in 1909.

New Arrivals

Words to Understand

assimilate   to make one kind of people more similar to another

epidemic   an event when a large number of people get a particular disease at the same time

exploit   to take advantage of something or someone, usually unfairly

missionary   a person who goes on a trip in order to promote a religion, usually Christianity

sovereignty   the power of a country to rule over a particular area

Arctic people had seen Europeans before the 1500s. Going back to medieval times, the Sami people of northern Scandinavia traded with their neighbors to the south. The Inuit in Canada and Greenland traded with Norse settlers. People in northern Siberia had relationships with Russian merchants.

The contact was limited, though, until about the 16th century. By then, Europeans were getting to explore new places. Adventurers, merchants, and **missionaries** all began to move into the Arctic. They were looking for new land, new resources, and new people to convert to Christianity. It started a tug-of-war over who had the "right" to the Arctic. Was it natives, or newcomers?

Early Explorations

Some Arctic explorers were merely curious about the region. Most, however, were more interested in the money that could be made from it. For one thing, the Arctic held valuable resources such as minerals, animal furs, and whale oil. In addition, Europeans were interested in finding a sea route across the Arctic Ocean. This would connect European trading markets to those in the Far East. The overland journey was long and difficult, so a sea passage across the Arctic Ocean might be faster and easier.

In 1576, an English explorer named Martin Frobisher sailed west to Canada. He was looking for a northwest passage through the Arctic Ocean. Frobisher was not successful, but his early voyage led the way for more. These journeys brought Arctic people into closer and more regular contact with white men than ever before.

In 1728, Russian explorers sailed across the Bering Strait to the west coast of North America. There, they **exploited** the native populations. The Russians forced them to work under cruel conditions to harvest the pelts from sea otters. The Russians then sold the pelts back home. The native people suffered greatly. Within a century, more than three-fourths of them had died. That didn't stop the Russians, though. By the 19th century, they had built a large fur trade in Alaska. Meanwhile, the English had established fur trading posts in Canada, notably Hudson's Bay. Europeans also built an industry based on hunting whales in the Arctic.

For many years, Russians demanded tribute, or yasak, *from Arctic people. This painting depicts furs being given to Russian visitors (right).*

There were some benefits to the interaction between European settlers and indigenous people. In North America, Europeans gave native people a new market for trading. It expanded their economy and gave them access to things they would not otherwise have had. In return for furs, the natives received items like cloth and guns. Goods like these were previously unknown to indigenous people and in some ways could make their lives easier.

On the other hand, the Europeans also introduced products such as tobacco and alcohol. These caused the Arctic people great harm in the long run. Even worse were the diseases carried by Europeans, such as smallpox, tuberculosis, mumps, influenza (flu), and measles, which were common in Europe. Europeans had faced these diseases for centuries and had developed some resistance to them. The native people had little immunity, though, and **epidemics** wiped out thousands of people.

The Case of Greenland

In many cases, Europeans treated native people poorly. An exception happened in Greenland. Norse immigrants had left Greenland in the 1400s. They returned three centuries later to try again. Unlike in other places, the settlers did not try to fully control native people, but instead tried to work with them. Certainly, the Europeans also promoted their own ideas, such as Christianity. However, they also showed respect for the native people. They allowed them to speak their own language. When European diseases became a threat, the government of Denmark stepped in to help. It only allowed one company to trade on Greenland, which helped reduce the contact with so many different people and diseases.

Life in Greenland

By the 1860s, Denmark let the native people of Greenland have some power to govern themselves. A century later, they got full representation in Denmark's national government. Finally, in 1978, Greenland was given complete home rule. Although Greenland is still part of the Kingdom of Denmark, it has the authority to make all its own decisions.

Depression and War

By the beginning of the 20th century, the Arctic economy was intertwined with their southern neighbors. The fur trade was booming. Arctic people had access to goods from Europe, Canada,

A group that traveled with Robert Peary to the North Pole in 1909 poses with flags of the nations on the trip, as well as societies that helped support his mission.

and America. On the surface, it seemed like a good deal, but it would have dire consequences.

Many native people tried hard to keep up with the demands of the new economy. They used up too many resources and abandoned their traditional ways. However, that economy would not last. By the late 1800s, overhunting of whales reduced their population and was no longer profitable. White men moved on,

The perils of Arctic sea travel were seen in this image of sailors chipping ice off their steel ship decks. Convoys of ships traveled the Arctic during World War II.

taking their money with them. Then, in the 1930s, the fur trade collapsed. Again, many immigrants simply left the area and went back where they had come from. Native people often no longer had the skills to go back to their traditional lives. They were forced to take low-paying jobs—if they could find them.

And then came World War II, which lasted from 1939 to 1945. When it ended, the world had become a very divided place. Technically, the nations around the globe were at peace. However, they now entered a new era called the "Cold War." During this time, the United States and the Soviet Union had a very uneasy relationship. The two countries had conflicting ideas about the economy and social organization. Neither one trusted the other. Making the whole situation worse was the threat of nuclear weapons. These were developed during World War II and were incredibly destructive.

The Arctic region now became a strategic military location. The United States was worried that the Soviets would try

Project Chariot

Nuclear weapons are terrible things, but maybe nuclear power can be used for good causes. That was what the United States wanted to do after World War II. In 1958, the US government planned Project Chariot. The project would use nuclear bombs to carve out a new harbor on the northwest coast of Alaska. The US government said the harbor could be used to export coal from nearby mines. That would help the economy in Alaska. There were several problems with this plan. The new harbor would be so far north that it would be frozen much of the year. During that time it would be useless for shipping. The plan also assumed native people would give up their traditional lifestyles. They would work as coal miners instead. Most troubling was the environmental damage. Nuclear explosions produce dangerous radioactive waste. It can kill people, animals, and plants. A small group of native people living in Point Hope, Alaska, protested the plan to create the harbor. In the end, the US government gave up on the idea.

to access America via the Arctic to launch an attack. To prevent this, the US set up military communication stations across the region. Central to this was the Distant Early Warning (DEW) line. Indigenous Arctic people were hired to help build this series of radar sites that stretched from Alaska, across Canada and into Greenland and Iceland. The sites would be able to detect Soviet airplanes or missiles, perhaps providing the United States enough time to defend itself. The increased military presence, however, created even more tension between white men and native peoples.

People with No Home

By the 1950s, trips into the North American Arctic were becoming even more common. They were also getting more intrusive. The Canadian government wanted to claim the far northern reaches of Arctic land. They wanted to establish **sovereignty**, meaning they had the right to control it. To do that, they needed people to live there. One solution was to relocate native Inuit people to these areas. (Most Inuit lived further south at the time.)

The Inuit were facing tough times at this point. They had learned to depend on the economy of white people. When it suffered, they had lost the ability to easily return to their traditional lives. The Canadian government thought relocating the Inuit would serve two purposes. One, the Inuit could resume their lifestyle, just in a different place. Two, the moves would help the government in its goal to own those lands.

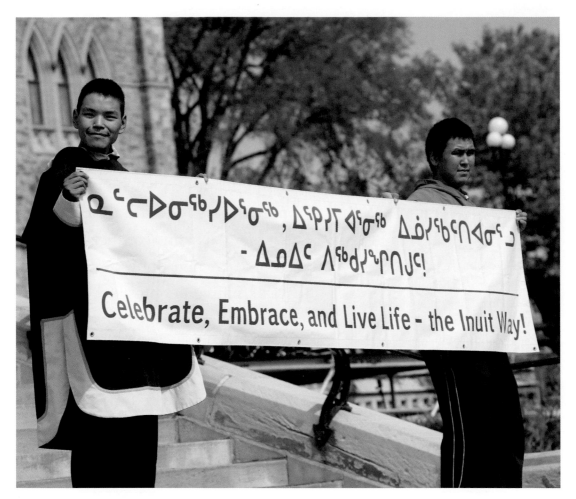

Suicide is a huge killer of native Arctic youth. This sign calls for help with this problem on World Suicide Prevention Day.

For the most part, these forced relocations were a disaster. The Canadian government did not take into account that Arctic lifestyles were not one-size-fits-all. The Inuit were moved hundreds or even thousands of miles from their homes. They were not prepared to adapt to different climates and landscapes. Overall, their situation got worse, not better.

The Sled Dog Slaughter

From the 1950s through the 1970s, the Royal Canadian Mounted Police (RCMP) shot and killed thousands of Husky sled dogs that belonged to the native Inuit. The RCMP said the act was necessary. They were trying to get rid of dogs that carried diseases, or that put people's safety in danger. However, many Inuit believed the killings happened for a different reason. They thought it was the government's way of trying to stamp out the traditional Inuit lifestyle. It would force the natives to adopt the ways of white people. Whatever the reason, the killings caused major injury to the Inuit population. Dogs helped them in hunting and travel, and they were often like family members.

Both the Canadian and US. governments also had another policy that hurt native people. They tried to **assimilate** them into the culture of white people. The governments taught beliefs and lifestyles that were common to Canadians and Americans but were very different from native peoples' traditional ideas. Often they came into conflict. Shamanism was frowned upon, for example. Instead, native peoples were encouraged to become Christians. In many cases, children were removed from their families and sent to schools far away. They were not allowed to speak their native languages. Many grew up without learning the skills that were traditional to their way of life.

The Russian Arctic

Across the ocean, Arctic people in Russia also suffered. By the late 1800s, Russian farmers and fur traders had taken over much of the northern land that had been used by native peoples. Then, in 1917, the government was overthrown during a revolution and Russia became the Soviet Union. A new economy based on communism went into effect. The major idea of communism was that no single person would own things or work for himself. Instead, everything was supposed to be done for the good of the whole country.

This new system was especially hard on Arctic people. Separated from the rest of the country, they were used to being independent. Some tried to resist, but their rebellions were put

These young Nenets women from northern Russia show off traditional ceremonial clothing, complete with a more Russian-like head scarf.

Oil pipelines cross several sensitive areas of Arctic land in the United States, Canada, and other nations. Keeping those pipelines secure is key to future Arctic safety.

down by the government. However, these people did have access to government benefits such as education and health care. Over time, the people became part of the Soviet lifestyle.

Then, in the early 1990s, the Soviet government collapsed. Communism was out. People had to depend more on themselves. Arctic people did not have the tools to adapt to this new structure. Many had lost their ability to live in traditional ways. The government that was supposed to help them was gone. Also, they were still relatively isolated from the rest of the country. Jobs were few and far between.

For almost five centuries, hundreds of thousands of Arctic natives had been misunderstood at best. In many cases they were unfairly used and even abused. First it was for furs, then whales, then gold. By the middle of the 20th century, the Arctic offered a new possibility. Vast reserves of oil lay beneath the ice. It could be used to fuel cars and power plants all over the world. Drilling for oil could mean an opportunity for Arctic people, but it also was a risk. Fortunately, by then the people of the Arctic had begun to stand together. They were working to protect their land and their lifestyles.

 # Text-Dependent Questions:

1. What was one major industry Europeans set up in the Arctic?

2. What was the purpose of the DEW line?

3. Why did the Canadian government force the Inuit to move to new areas?

 # Research Project

Whaling was a way of life for many Arctic people. Research how Arctic people traditionally hunted whales, and how they became involved in the whaling industries of Europeans and Americans.

Oil barrels left to rust and decay on the Arctic shoreline are just one visible indication of the negative impact that the 20th and 21st centuries are having on the Arctic.

Steps Forward, Steps Back

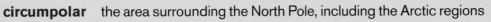
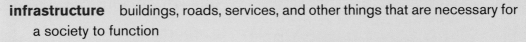

4

Words to Understand

activist   someone who works for a particular cause

circumpolar   the area surrounding the North Pole, including the Arctic regions

erode   to break down or wear away

infrastructure   buildings, roads, services, and other things that are necessary for a society to function

toxin   poison

The problems of the 20th century came with one big benefit. They made Arctic people find ways to come together. More than ever before, native people have the knowledge and tools to fight for their rights. However, pressure on the Arctic is also greater than ever before. Environmental problems are a big threat. The region itself is also at the center of political battles around the globe.

Finding a Voice

People native to the Arctic have never had the same priorities as other countries. They were not prepared for the problems thrust upon them by other societies. Yet, being able to adapt is key to Arctic survival. In the 1960s and 1970s Arctic people tried several ways to establish and protect their rights. One of the first was in Alaska in 1962. A newspaper called the *Tundra Times* started to report on issues that affected native people. A few years later, in 1966, a group was formed called the Alaska Federation of Natives. Its purpose was to help members reclaim land that the state government had taken from them.

Within a decade, similar movements were springing up. In the early 1970s, the Inuit in Greenland began pushing for "home rule." This would give them the power to make their own decisions. Denmark (which controlled Greenland)

Nunavut

In 1993, Canada made a step toward giving power to the native Inuit people. It established a new territory in northeastern Canada called Nunavut. As of 2016, about 37,000 people live there. Most of them are Inuit. Under the agreement, the native people can hunt, fish, and use the land in Nunavut according to their ancient traditions. They are allowed to share in any profits that come from oil drilling. The Inuit also received money to help build their **infrastructure**, such as schools and roads, and to set up their own independent government. Creating Nunavut was a bold effort, but there are still problems. It is hard to find somewhere to live, and things are expensive. Many young people do not graduate from high school and have trouble finding jobs. However, the area also has important natural resources. Those may help the economy over time.

Russian foreign minister Sergei Lavrov joined US Secretary of State John Kerry (third from left) at a 2013 Arctic Council meeting.

gave home rule to the people in 1979. Meanwhile, people from Greenland, Canada, and Alaska suggested having a meeting. It would bring together native people from several Arctic countries. In 1977, they held the first Inuit **Circumpolar** Conference.

In 1996, the Arctic Council was established. It has members from all eight countries that own land in the Arctic. The council organizes studies on issues that are important in the Arctic. Some of these are transportation, oil and gas exploration, and climate change.

Polar bears and other animals sometimes have to negotiate huge mounds of trash and discarded equipment. Some cleanup is underway, but there is much more to do.

Environmental Changes

People in the Arctic are better represented than they used to be. Now they must deal with the changes affecting the region. Perhaps the biggest one is climate change. Global warming is making the Arctic ice melt faster than ever before. The ice freezes later and later each year. Each year, more of the ice doesn't come back at all. There is less time to go out on the ice to hunt, and it's more dangerous. Every year, hunters die falling through thin ice that used to be solid. As the sea level rises from the melting ice, it's also starting to **erode** coastlines. Homes and even entire towns are getting washed out.

Pollution is another problem. A main cause of global warming is from burning fossil fuels such as oil and coal. This produces carbon dioxide. Carbon dioxide then gets absorbed into water, making it more acidic. This is happening everywhere, but it's especially bad in the Arctic. The water there is becoming unsafe for fish and other animals. Ocean currents also carry pollution from other places and dump it in the Arctic. Even though the Arctic is warming up, it's still cold compared to most places. That means that it takes much longer for pollutants to break down. Pollution is more concentrated in Arctic waters than in other places.

Toxins also build up in the meat and fatty tissues of animals that Arctic people depend on for food. In some places, people face a terrible choice.

Leaving Home

The tiny town of Kivalina, Alaska, has become a symbol of the problems facing the Arctic. Traditionally, the native people have hunted bowhead whales that pass by their shores. But global warming has thinned the ice. It's pushed the whales too far from shore. Other species, from caribou to fish, are also dwindling. Hunger is a big concern for many of the town's 400 citizens. The ice also used to protect the town. It was a barrier against storms and waves coming off the sea. Without it, the whole town is vulnerable. By the late 1990s, the town's residents knew they had to move. In 2008, they filed a lawsuit against major oil companies. They claimed the companies had contributed to the problem of global warming. They should take responsibility by giving Kivalina's residents money to move. The town lost the case, but that's only one problem. Global warming is affecting the whole Arctic. Finding a new home has been difficult.

If they follow their traditional diet, they could be eating a lot of poison. If they switch to a Western diet, they'll be getting unhealthy foods that could cause other problems.

Just as there are fewer food sources, there are also more people. The population of the Arctic is growing faster than ever before. Arctic people are being forced to depend more on im-

A signpost in Barrow, Alaska, one of the northernmost US settlements, points the way to both poles and some major cities in the "Lower 48" and elsewhere.

New meets old: Snowmobiles are popular transportation options for Alaskans. The warmer summer and spring months are a good time to see new models.

ported Western food. Prices for items like these are extremely high in the Arctic. That puts even more strain on people who have trouble finding jobs. Even those who do find food through traditional hunting face criticism. Many animal rights **activists** object to killing endangered species, such as polar bears, which causes even more tension.

The Race for Resources

The Arctic holds vast reserves of natural resources. Oil, natural gas, coal, copper, uranium, and even diamonds can be found in its land and waters. Oil wells in the Arctic already produce a significant amount of the world's supply. Now, as the ice melts, places that were too difficult to reach before could become accessible. The United States is considering whether to increase oil drilling in the Arctic. Russia is also making aggressive moves into the area.

The "should-we-or-shouldn't-we" debate is fierce. Oil companies see another source of profit. Governments see a way to provide fuel to their citizens. Arctic people could also benefit from increased oil drilling. For one thing, it would provide jobs. The money earned from exports could help build roads, schools, and hospitals.

On the flip side, more drilling would certainly put new strains on the environment. There would be more people, more roads, and more buildings. In addition, now that the ice is melting, traveling through the Arctic Ocean has become even easier. That means more traffic that could hurt the environment. An even bigger danger is the risk of an oil spill. In 1989, the oil tanker Exxon Valdez ripped open on a reef off the coast of Alaska. It spilled millions of gallons of oil and killed millions of animals. Oil is very difficult to clean up, especially when it's mixed with water. Almost 30 years later, the water is still contaminated with oil from the spill.

Moving Forward

Technology has made the world a smaller place. Once, traveling across the Arctic was incredibly difficult. It's still a challenge today, but it's not quite as hard. Snowmobiles can go much faster and farther than skiers or sled dogs. Powerful ships can break through several feet of ice in the water. The Arctic is still remote, but it's more connected than ever before.

Oil spills are dangerous to people, but they also have a devastating effect on wildlife. Here, a worker tries to help an oil-covered seabird.

People in Chukotka, Russia, got together to make a plan to preserve an important stopping place for walrus migration.

The electronic revolution has not bypassed the Arctic, either. First, it was television. Then it was the Internet. These have exposed native people to cultures that are very different from theirs. Of course, it's not automatically bad to enjoy other cultures. However, there are some definite downsides. Most young people prefer to watch TV and movies from Western culture. As a result, their native languages are dying out. Traditions like storytelling are also suffering.

The vast majority of people who now live in the Arctic aren't native. They've arrived just within the last few generations. More often than not, they do not directly depend on the Arctic's resources to survive. Instead, their jobs are focused on harvesting those resources for people in other parts of the world.

Climate change effects

Companies and countries both are staking a claim in the Far North. In 2007, the crew from a Russian submarine even planted a flag at the bottom of the Arctic Ocean. With that, Russia said it was claiming the right to much of the land in the Arctic. (Other countries protested the move.) Still, plans for new development will undoubtedly change the Arctic.

Greenland is one such place where traditional ways are conflicting with modern progress. There, the traditional seal-hunting economy is dying out. The demand is for different types of workers, such as people who work on oil rigs or do construction. Still, many lifelong hunters and fishermen in Greenland are not willing to switch jobs. Living off the land is not simply a way to feed themselves—it's a big part of their overall culture.

Yet there are encouraging signs, too. One example comes from the Russian region of Chukotka. In the late 1990s, people living there noticed that the walrus population was suffering. Melting ice had pushed the animals farther out to sea and the local people could no longer hunt them. To coax the walrus back to shore, the people created walrus haul-outs. Basically, these are

The future of the Arctic and its people is a bit more uncertain than it once was. The modern world continues to change traditional life.

"rest stops" for traveling walrus. The walrus came ashore again, and the people were able to hunt them. To follow tradition, and not scare the walrus away, they used spears instead of guns.

The current state of the Arctic is defined by the struggle between traditional and modern ways. Certainly, there is no going back to the past. The Arctic will never again be a place that is untouched by the rest of the world. What's not certain is what the future will bring, and how it will affect the people who live there. Fortunately, Arctic people are survivors. The question is how they will do it now.

 # Text-Dependent Questions:

1. What is one way the Nunavut agreement was designed to help the Inuit people?

2. How does melting ice affect Arctic hunters?

3. Give one example of how technology has changed life in the Arctic.

 # Research Project

Iqaluit is the largest city in Nunavut, the Canadian territory established for Inuit people. Find out more about Iqaluit, such as its main industries and cultural events.

FIND OUT MORE

Websites

www.firstpeoplesofcanada.com/fp_groups/fp_inuit3.html
Learn more about the history and habits of the Inuit of Canada at this site.

wwf.panda.org/what_we_do/where_we_work/arctic/arctic_peoples/
Read about some of the things native Arctic people are doing to protect their environment and lifestyle.

naturalhistory.si.edu/arctic/html/resources_faq.html
Check out this site to find answers to some interesting questions about the Arctic.

kinooze.com/inuit-people-of-the-arctic/
Read about the life of a modern-day Inuit boy.

Books

Arnez, Lynda. *Native Peoples of the Arctic.* New York: Gareth Stevens, 2016.

Doherty, Craig and Katherine Doherty. *Arctic Peoples.* New York: Chelsea House, 2008.

Green, Jen. *Hands-On History! Eskimo, Inuit, Saami & Arctic Peoples.* Helotes, TX: Armadillo, 2014.

Qitsualik-Tinsley, Rachel and Sean Qitsualik-Tinsley. *Skraelings: Clashes in the Old Arctic.* Iqualit, NU: Inhabit Media, 2014.

Taylor, Barbara. *Arctic & Antarctic.* New York: DK Eyewitness Books, 2012.

SERIES GLOSSARY OF KEY TERMS

circumpolar: the area surrounding the North Pole, including the Arctic regions

Cold War: when nations are openly hostile toward each other while not resorting to physical warfare

continental shelf: the relatively shallow seabed surrounding a continent; the edge of a continent as it slopes down into the sea

floe: an ice sheet floating in the water

indigenous: native or original to a particular place

meteorology: the study of weather

pelts: furred animal skins

permafrost: a layer of soil that stays frozen all year long

province: an area in Canada with its own name and government, similar to a state

subsistence: a basic, minimal way of living, with only things that are necessary to survive

sustainable: something that can be maintained or practiced for a long duration without negative effects

taiga: a biome that includes the forest of mostly evergreen trees found in the southern Arctic regions

territorial waters: the parts of an ocean over which a country has control

tundra: a type of biome in very cold areas characterized by limited plant growth, frozen soil, and low rainfall

INDEX

PHOTO CREDITS

ABOUT THE AUTHOR

Diane Bailey has written more than 50 nonfiction books for kids and teens, on topics ranging from science to sports to celebrities. She also works as a freelance editor, helping authors who write novels for children and young adults. Diane has two sons and two dogs, and lives in Kansas.